In-the-Bag STORIES

Object Talks for Children

by Louise Kohr

ISBN 0-87403-758-1
©1990. The STANDARD PUBLISHING Company.
Division of STANDEX INTERNATIONAL Corporation.
Printed in U.S.A.   14-02862

To
the greatest of God's gifts,
besides His Son,
children

Contents

Introduction

These stories have an object or objects in a paper bag to use in telling the stories. They help hold children's interest and attention in these days of visual communication.

These stories were written for children's church or the children's time at the regular worship service. The objects are easily obtainable at home or from a local discount store.

A good story is a good story wherever it's told. These in-the-bag stories have a point children will be able to grasp, and they will not be entirely lost time for the adult listener.

The eight-year-old child is the median age targeted by the author. You may have to simplify the stories or raise them to the general level of your group. You should know better than anyone else the abilities of your listeners. These stories are merely outlines to follow.

If toddlers fail to understand, they will still benefit from sitting and listening to the worship service. *Never* underestimate a child's understanding, even though he or she may seem to be concentrating more on climbing the pulpit.

I hope you will find inspiration as you work with one of the most important segments of the church with these stories. The telling of them to children is a priceless privilege. Treasure it.

Belonging

door key
jar lid
flashlight battery

Let's see what we have in the bag. Hmmm! What is this? A key, es. What does it belong to? A lock, the lock of a door or chest. If ou have no key, is the lock any good? No. To open a lock you ust have a key. To use a key, you must have a lock.

And what have we here? A lid? What does it belong to? A jar, es. Without it, things would spill out of the jar.

And this? What is this? A battery. What does it belong to? A ashlight? It might. Or it could belong to a toy car or a small electric ppliance like a toothbrush. It could belong to several things.

Now, who and what do you belong to? Your family, of course. nd you belong to your class at church. Maybe you belong to a eighborhood ball team or the Cub Scouts or Brownies. There are lso many other things you may belong to, such as first or second rade.

Even though you belong to many things, you must never forget at first of all you belong to God. Your belonging to Him should set pattern for the life you live and the kind of child you are.

God wants to be a guide to all those who belong to Him. We ust always seek His guidance. Remember that this week, will ou?

You belong. Be glad.

"These things belong to us and our older children for ever. It is so we will do everything in these teachings" (Deuteronomy 29:29).

Follow the Leader

needle and thread
magnet

Good morning boys and girls! Do you ever play "Follow the Leader?" It's fun, isn't it?

Now what is in the bag this morning? What is this? A needle, yes, it's a needle.

What is a needle good for? For sewing. Right?

And what is this? A spool of thread. Right! And what is it good for? It is for sewing, too, isn't it?

Now, tell me, is the needle any good for sewing without thread? No. But you can pick it up like this with a magnet. Or your mother can maybe take a splinter out of your finger with it. But it isn't any good for sewing without thread, is it?

But when your mother puts thread in the needle, like this, *(One of the older children may like to thread the needle for you. Be sure to have a large-eyed one.)* then the thread will follow the needle and do what she wants it to.

Now all of us have someone we admire, someone we would like to follow, to be like.

There is one very special leader for all of us. God sent His Son, Jesus, to guide us through life the way the needle leads the thread. If we follow Him, as He has asked us to do, we will be the kind of man or woman, boy or girl, He wants us to be. We will know where He wants us to go and we will do the job He means for us to do.

Next time you see your mother or grandmother threading a needle, will you think about Jesus and following Him?

See you next Sunday.

"Follow me" (Matthew 4:19).

The Church

building blocks

Give each child a block. Then ask them to show you what they can build with it.

You can't build anything with just one block, can you? But if all of you put your blocks together, you could build something. O.K. Let's put them together and build a church here on this table. Come, add your block.

Do you like to come to church? That's why we have a church school, isn't it? To learn about God.

Our church school is like the one you have built with blocks. One of us alone could not make a church school. It cannot be put together with one brick or one person. It has to be built by all of us together, each one doing his or her part.

Maybe you can sing. Maybe you can pass out the books. Maybe you can invite someone to come to church school with you next Sunday.

It was Christian people who felt the need of a church here. They wanted a place in which to worship, so each gave some money for a board or a brick. It was his or her part toward the building of this church.

But not in bricks alone. Now each person must continue to give to God's house so that it may be a place of inspiration and service to all. Do you know what those words mean? They mean helping others.

God has asked us to do this. The church needs many things: prayer, singing, money, someone to keep it clean, and faithful members to come every Sunday to say thank you to God for all His goodness.

He is glad that you are here today. I hope that you will be here next Sunday, too. See you then.

> "Let's go to the temple of the Lord" (Psalm 122:1).

God's Gifts

peanuts

I want to tell you a story this morning about a boy and his mother who were abducted by some men called Nightriders. They were taken by force from the place where they lived to be sold into slavery.

The boy's mother was never seen again, but some friends finally found the boy and traded an old horse for him. They returned him to people who loved him.

His captors hadn't taken good care of the boy. He wasn't very strong and couldn't work much. He spent his time wandering about the farm and hills where he lived, getting to know God's world.

What a wondrous place it was. He collected flowers and strange weeds. He worked his way through high school, and in college he earned a degree. After college he was offered a place to live where he could help his own people, who were black. That was what he wanted to do more than anything else.

The soil where this man lived was poor. The people who lived there could raise peanuts and a few sweet potatoes, but there wasn't enough grass for them to have a cow. Most were so poor their children never had milk. Peanuts!

Did you know you can make milk out of them? No one else did either until this man, George Washington Carver, experimented and found a way to do it. He discovered that peanuts were rich in protein which helps boys and girls to grow. He found two hundred ways to use peanuts!

Peanuts are a gift from God, and Carver made them gifts of life. Think of that the next time you munch a peanut butter sandwich!

"The heavens tell the glory of God. And the skies announce what his hands have made" (Psalm 19:1).

10

Footprints

pictures of animal tracks

(Lincoln's birthday)

Good morning, boys and girls! Could you follow an animal by its tracks? Would you know what animal you were following? What kind of animal would you say left these? A cat of some kind?

Did you know that people too leave tracks wherever they go? They leave them in many ways.

Did you leave a smile where you were yesterday? The day before? Was someone happier because you went where you did? Your smile was a kind of track you left behind.

Whose birthday do (did) we celebrate this week? Abraham Lincoln's. That's right. Lincoln left footprints in our country's history.

Let me tell you a story about another kind of "tracks" Lincoln once left when he was a boy living in Indiana. It happened one day when he played a joke on his stepmother.

While she was at a neighbor's, Lincoln took his little brother, whose feet were muddy from the puddle by the cow tank, and turned him upside down. He told his brother to hold his legs stiff.

Then Abe "walked" his brother right up the wall, across the low ceiling, and down the wall on the other side. But when his stepmother saw the steps across the ceiling, she put her apron over her head and her shoulders began to shake. Lincoln thought she was crying and felt sorry for what he had done because he loved her very much.

His stepmother wasn't angry though, she was laughing under her apron. But she did make Lincoln whitewash the ceiling to clean off the footprints.

Remember you, too, leave a kind of "tracks" wherever you go. Leave good ones that will please Jesus.

"How beautiful are the feet of the one who says . . . 'Your God is king' " (Isaiah 52:7).

11

Books

black-bound Bible
paper-back Bible
small red New Testament
storybook

Good morning. What do I have in the bag today? Let's see. A Bible. Yes. And this? This is another Bible. This, too.

Do they all say the same thing? Well, they are all the story of God's love for you and me, but some of them may say it a little differently.

Did you know that more Bibles are sold than any other book ever written? We all need to read God's Book so we can know how He wants us to live.

(*Take out a storybook*)

And what is this? A storybook, yes. Do you have a favorite storybook? Does your mother read it to you sometimes?

There are many stories in the Bible. Stories of Jesus: how He taught, how He healed people, made the blind to see, and the lame to walk.

Do you remember the story of baby Moses and how his mother hid him in a basket to keep him safe? Do you think your mother would hide you to keep you safe from harm?

Do you remember the story of the boy who shared his lunch so Jesus could bless it and feed thousands of hungry people?

Do you remember the story of David and the giant and how the shepherd boy was not afraid because he trusted God?

That is why we come to church on Sunday morning, to hear the beautiful stories God has for us in the Bible. His book may come to be your favorite storybook. The Bible is a guidebook to teach us how to live a good life. Remember that, will you?

"Let the teaching of Christ live in you richly" (Colossians 3:16).

Happiness

ball

Good morning! I want to talk to you today about happiness. How many of you have heard the prayer, "Our Father who art in Heaven?" Who can tell me what comes next? Good!

Can anyone tell me who gave us this prayer? Yes, Jesus did. And if we live the way it tells us to, we can be happy. God, our Father in Heaven, wants us to be happy.

How do we know this? His book, the Bible, tells us so. In it the word happy is used about fifty times, and joy, another word that stands for happiness, is in the Bible about a hundred and fifty times. Isn't that proof enough that God wants His children to be happy?

Now happiness is like this ball. I bounce it and what happens? It comes right back to me. Like this! One of the very best ways ever discovered to be happy, is to make someone else happy. Try it. The joy you give to another person bounces right back at you like this ball.

If you look in a mirror and smile, your face will smile right back at you. If there's happiness in your smile, it will show in your face for everyone to see.

Now, let's all stand up and turn around and let others see the happiness that is in us. That will make God happy, too.

"Happy are those who are helped by the God of Jacob" (Psalm 146:5).

Cookies

cookies

I want to talk to you this morning about friends. *(Take a cookie out of the bag and start to eat it as you talk)*

Do you have a friend? A special friend? At school? Or in your neighborhood? Do you have a friend here at church who is special? Are you happy when you are with that friend? Why? Because that friend shares with you? *(Keep eating)*

There used to be a little song we sang that went like this:

> Friends, friends, friends.
> I have a friend I love.
> I love my friend
> And he loves me.
> I help my friend
> And he helps me.
> Friends, friends, friends.

(Talk to the children about friends. Try to get them to respond while you continue to eat cookies from the bag.)

If they mention sharing, that's good. If not, say, "Do you think of me as a friend? I hope you do. What do you think about me eating cookies all by myself? Do you think I should offer to share with you if I am your friend? A good friend would do that, wouldn't she? Should a good friend share? Of course. *(Pass the cookies around)*

The church has friends all 'round the world. Jesus said, "Go ye into all the world." That means He wants us to share with friends nearby. He wants us to share, too, with friends in faraway places. He wants us to tell others everywhere of His love. Remember that wherever you go.

"A friend loves you all the time" (Proverbs 17:17).

14

Learning to Do

squeaky whistle

Good morning, boys and girls. I would like to talk to you today about learning to do things.

Is there something you would like very much to learn to do? What would you like to learn to do? Something maybe your big brother or sister does, or maybe your mother or dad? Something you see bigger boys and girls doing? Something that may look easy when someone else does it.

I want to tell you about a boy named Tommy who wanted to learn to whistle. His dad could whistle. The boy who delivered the paper could whistle. Even one of the boys in his own class could whistle. But when Tommy tried, nothing would come out but a whish.

His mother knew how much Tommy wanted to whistle, so she bought him a whistle at the store. It sounded like this. *(Blow your squeaky whistle)* But Tommy didn't want a store whistle. He wanted to whistle himself, but he couldn't.

Someone told him to eat a sour pickle, and it would pucker up his lips the right way to whistle. He ate a very sour pickle. It puckered his lips, but he still couldn't whistle.

He tried and tried, and then one day when he was almost ready to give up, he puckered his lips and out came a whistle. It wasn't a very big one, but he knew that if he kept trying it would get better.

Sometimes things don't happen just when we want them to. We have to keep on trying.

Did you ever have a problem like Tommy's? If you haven't, you will sometime. When you do, just remember to keep trying. The hard things are often the most important.

"You must hold on, so you can do what God wants" (Hebrews 10:36).

The Secret

brown bulb

Do you like secrets? They're fun, aren't they? Can you keep one?

What do I have here? A bulb, yes! Just a little brown bulb. But it holds a secret in its heart; a secret it cannot keep long when the rains wake it and the sun warms it. What a wonder it is, this little brown bulb. It will burst into beauty when planted. Only God could create such a wonder.

It isn't going to stay just a dry, brown bulb. It is going to grow, to burst into bloom.

You are something like this bulb. In your heart are many beautiful thoughts, much kindness and the desire to share happiness.

Who hid the secret in the heart of the bulb? Yes, God did. He put loving thoughts, kindness and the desire to share happiness in your heart, too.

But just a minute. Will the bulb bloom without God's care? No. It needs the sunshine and the rain He sends to make it burst into bloom.

You need Him, too. Always remember that. You are growing every day in His care and love. And even if you are not very big, you can make this a better world and a happier place by being the child He wants you to be. Try to remember that.

"I have taken your words to heart" (Psalm 119:11).

Trees

leaves from various trees

Good morning, everyone! How good to see you all here today.

One of God's greatest gifts to us is trees. In the bag this morning I have leaves from several trees. Can any of you tell me what tree this leaf comes from? This one? What kind of trees do you have in your yard? An apple tree? An elm? A maple?

Did your dad plant one of the trees in your yard? If he did, he was helping God to make a more beautiful world, wasn't he?

Some leaves are like this one, long and narrow. Some are separated into parts like this one. Some are almost heart shaped. All are wondrously made and shaped for its own tree.

Do you know what leaves do for a tree? They feed it. The leaves catch the sunshine and the rain and send them down through the branches of the tree to its roots. The roots reach deep into the earth to hold the tree steady.

And what do trees do for us? They give us fruit, yes. They give us wood for our homes. We can build furniture with it or burn it in our fireplaces. They give us shade and beauty. And they help clean the air.

Trees make nesting places for birds. Climbing places for boys and girls. And they hold swings.

If the world had to live without trees, it would be a far less beautiful place. You can think of a tree as a pattern. Like it, you can grow tall and strong in the sunshine and rain of God's love.

"Happy is the person who . . . loves the Lord's teachings . . . He is strong, like a tree . . ." (Psalm 1:1-3).

The Children's Friend

bag of jelly beans

I have a surprise for you today. *(Give each child a few jelly beans)* Then ask the children if they like jelly beans.

Good, aren't they? What colors are yours? And what colors did you get? Are yours good, too? What color do you like best?

It doesn't matter much what color they are, does it? That's right. They're all good.

God's love is something like that. He loves children of all colors. When I was a child in Sunday school, we used to sing a song about God's love for children. It went like this:

> Jesus loves the little children,
> All the children of the world.
> Red and yellow, black and white,
> They are precious in His sight.
> Jesus loves the little children of the world.

Do you sing that song in your Sunday-school class? If not, ask your teacher if she will sing it for you.

But whether you sing it or not, it is still true. Jesus does love children everywhere; tall ones, short ones, fat ones, thin ones, children of all colors.

And know something else, He wants you to love them too.

Will you try to remember that this week? Look around you for some way to show your love for other children.

"You will always owe love to each other" (Romans 13:8).

Candles

eight small pink candles
one tall red candle

Let's see what we have in the bag this morning. Candles! Pink candles and a red one. How many pink candles? Eight, to flicker and shine. I like candles, don't you?

Let me tell you a story about candles this morning. A woman went to a store one day and said, "I would like eight candles."

"Oh," said the clerk, "a birthday?"

The mother smiled happily. "Eight years old," she said. "It seems like only yesterday that she was spilling cereal all over the place. They do grow so fast."

"Everyone loves a birthday," the woman behind the counter said as she wrapped the pink candles in tissue paper.

Then the mother saw a tall, shiny red candle on the shelf. "Oh," she said, "how lovely. I will take that one, too."

The clerk wrapped it in tissue paper.

At home the mother put the pink candles on a frosty white cake. The tall one she set in the middle of the table.

But when she tried to light the red candle, it wouldn't light. The candle was afraid that burning would make it stand crooked, and it didn't want its wax to run down its shiny red sides.

It was almost time for the guests to arrive, so the mother put the red candle away in a drawer. But when the candle in the dark drawer heard the children laughing and singing around the little pink candles, it wished it had let its light shine.

The next time the mother tried to light it, the tall red candle flickered for a moment and then let its light shine brightly.

A candle that doesn't shine isn't much good, is it?

"You are the light that gives light to the world" (Matthew 5:14).

Mother's Day

colored paper

Good morning. Tell me, who got your breakfast this morning? Who combed your hair? Who had your clothes ready for church and helped you find clean socks? Who listens when you have something to talk about?

What day is this? Mother's Day. What is Mother's Day? It's a day set aside to show our mothers how much we love them.

How can we do that? By honoring them. By obeying and being the kind of boy or girl they want us to be. On Mother's Day we wear flowers to show that we love them. Sometimes we give them gifts of flowers. But all of us can give our mothers the greatest gift of all—love.

Some people can take a piece of paper and make it look like a flower. I have some sheets of colored paper in the bag. I am going to give each of you one sheet. And I want you to take it with you and make a flower out of it, or draw flowers on it. Then I want you to write "I love you" on your flower or drawing and give it to your mother with a hug.

The flowers you make may not be the most beautiful ones in the world, but your mothers will think they are because they come from you. Mothers are like that.

A Happy Mother's Day to your mothers and to you.

"Honor your father and mother . . . " (Ephesians 6:2).

Pictures

a wallet containing snapshots

(Take out the wallet)

Does your mother or dad have a wallet with pictures in it? Does your grandmother carry your picture around to show to anyone who will look at it? Pretty proud of you, isn't she?

Because your parents and grandparents love you very much, they will say, "This is when he or she was four years old. And look at this one, see how much he or she is growing."

Does your mother or father carry a picture of Jesus in his or her purse? No, they don't. You see, they don't need to carry His picture in their purse or wallet. They have their own picture of Him in their hearts.

Your mother has a picture of you and of other loved ones in her heart, too, of course. But you are always changing, growing. This year's school picture shows you much bigger than you were last year, doesn't it?

Jesus never changes. He is the same yesterday, today, and forever.

People have different ideas of what He looks like, and none of the artists who have painted Him ever really saw Jesus.

But it doesn't matter what you think He looks like, so long as you carry His picture in your heart and remember to love Him. He is always near. Remember that.

"Jesus Christ is the same yesterday, today, and forever" (Hebrews 13:8).

Let It Shine

candle
matches

(Light the candle)

What do I have here? Yes, a candle. Do candles send out a big light? No, they don't make a very big light. But have you ever had the power go off and had to light a candle to find your way? Did you ever use a candle at camp or anytime when you had no other light?

Candles can light up dark corners, can't they? And what else do candles do? They mark birthdays on a cake, don't they?

Candles are something like smiles. A smile lights up a face like a candle lights a dark room. Have you ever thought of that?

Did you ever do something you were sorry for, and when you told your mother you were sorry, her face lit up with a smile? She wasn't angry. A smile can make things right again, can't it?

God is like that. When you do something you are truly sorry for, and tell Him you are sorry, you can be sure He is smiling too.

Did you ever speak kindly to a new child in your school, or someone who is lonely, and see the "candle" of a smile light their faces? Try it.

No, candles aren't big, and neither are you. But you can set lights to glowing if you will remember to try. There is a children's song about it:

> This little light of mine,
> I'm going to let it shine.

Do you know that song? Will you try shining your little light this week and let me know what happens? Go and shine!

"You should be a light for other people" (Matthew 5:16).

22

Color

a box of crayons

Do you have a box of crayons? A coloring book? Do you like to color pictures?

God does. He paints them all the time. Look about you and see. Wouldn't this be a dull world without flowers, birds, trees and the sky?

(If time permits, give each child a sheet of paper and ask him or her to draw a rainbow)

Can you draw a rainbow? God can. Would you like to hear a story about a rainbow?

A little girl once sat beside her mother on her bed. The doctor had said her mother was very sick.

The little girl was frightened. What if something should happen to her mother. She didn't know what she would do.

A nurse came in to take the mother's temperature. The little girl moved to the window to wait. She looked up and saw a rainbow in the sky.

How beautiful! she thought. *If God can paint a rainbow in the sky, He can make my mother well.* And suddenly the little girl was no longer afraid. God loved her. He loved her mother, too, and would make her well.

And He did.

This kind of believing is called faith. It is knowing that God cares and watches over us. He has said, "Believe in me."

The rainbow He paints in the sky is His promise of loving care. Your mother kisses you as a sign of her love for you. God's rainbow is like that. It's a sign and a promise. Always remember that, will you?

"The Lord has kept all the good promises he gave . . . " (1 Kings 8:56).

Map

Bible
map

I want to ask you a riddle this morning. "What does your mother have that no one else anywhere has?"

Think real hard. Give up? The answer is you!

(Take out the map) Do you know what this is? A map. That's right. What is it for? To show the way. And what is this? A Bible!

Now, why is a map like a Bible? Because they both show the way.

Once a man was going to build a house. He didn't bother to get a plan. He said he could build a house all by himself.

It was an awful mess. The windows were crooked and the doors wouldn't shut because the roof came down too far. The house had to be torn down and built all over again.

The Bible tells us how to build useful and happy lives, the way God wants them to be. He doesn't want us to build just any old way like the man in our story built his house. If we have problems building our lives, He is always near and ready to help us if we ask Him.

God has a plan for your life. He wants to guide and help you. If you remember to follow Him, you will never get lost on the road. He will help you build your "house" strong and straight. God says, "Call upon me. I will hear." Isn't it wonderful to know that?

"Let me tell you a riddle" (Judges 14:12).

Asking

poster: "Teach Us to Prae"
eraser

Can anyone tell me what this says? "Teach us to Pray."

What is prayer? What does it mean to pray. That's right. It is talking to God. He is our father in Heaven, and He wants us to talk to Him. He has told us this in His Book, the Bible.

But prayer shouldn't be just asking for things. It should be thanking God too. Thanking Him for all His blessings: for His Son, Jesus, for our families, our homes, food, and warmth. There are more things to be thankful for than we can name.

Once the disciples asked Jesus to teach them to pray, and He taught them the prayer that begins, "Our Father in heaven." In it we praise Him, we ask His blessings, and we thank Him.

(*Point out that "Pray" is misspelled*)

When we do something wrong and are truly sorry, God will forgive us. We only have to tell Him we're sorry and He will wipe it out—like this. (*Erase the "E" and make it "Y"*)

Remember, when we do something we are sorry for, God forgives us.

"Forgive the sins we have done" (Matthew 6:12).

Storytelling

long pencil
short stubby pencil

Do you like to read or listen to a good story? Most children do. That is the way Indians taught their children the history of their people. They would tell them stories. This was before there were schools for Indians.

Did you ever stop to think that what you did today might make an interesting story to some child in a far-off land? That each day you live is like turning another page in a book about you? Did you ever think that someday you might grow up to be full of stories children might like to hear?

I have here two pencils, a tall one and a very short one. One of them is the grandfather and the other is the boy. Which of these pencils do you think is the boy pencil? Which the grandfather?

(Ask the question until someone comes up with the answer that the little pencil is the boy.)

Then say, no, the grandfather is the short one. You see, his life has been mostly written. But this tall pencil stands for the boy whose life is still ahead. He has a lot of pages still to write.

Have you thought what you might like to do with your life? You, and you only, can make a beautiful story of it.

(You might want to give each child a new pencil, perhaps one with a Bible verse on it.)

"The little child began to grow up. He became stronger and wiser, and God's blessings were with him" (Luke 2:40).

Psalms (Songs)

**Bible
slingshot**

A long time ago, before Jesus was born, there was a shepherd boy named David.

David had a harp on which he played music. It wasn't the big kind of harp you may have seen, but was small enough to carry with him into the hills. And while he watched his sheep, David played his harp.

He thought of God's goodness in making the sun to shine and the rain to fall, because they made the grass grow for the sheep to eat.

David thought of the beauty of the sky and the world about him.

There were lions in the hills in those days. Sometimes they came out to catch a sheep. David was not afraid. He knew that God kept watch over him while he watched over the sheep. He had a sling-shot and knew how to use it to protect the flock.

David made up songs about God and His care and sang them as he played his harp. There is a whole book of these songs in our Bible. It's called Psalms. David wrote many of them. You will find the Psalms by opening God's Book in the middle. The words of some of David's songs are beautiful. One of his best known songs is the one that begins: "The Lord is my shepherd."

Do you know the song, "Praise Him, Praise Him?" Let's sing it together.

> "Praise Him, Praise Him,
> All ye little children,
> God is love, God is love.
> Praise Him, Praise Him
> All ye little children,
> God is love, God is love."

"Thank the Lord because he is good" (Psalm 107:1).

Symbols

ring
flag
candle

Do you know what a symbol is? It is something that stands for something else.

Does your mother wear a ring like this on a finger of her left hand? That ring stands for the marriage of your father and mother. It is a symbol of their love for one another and for you.

The flag is a symbol in the same way. It stands for the brave men who have kept our country free. The colors of red, white and blue are symbols too. The red stands for courage or bravery. The blue stands for truth. And the white is the symbol for purity.

The stars are symbols for the individual states of our country. We think of the flag as beautiful because it stands for our country.

The flag is a symbol of love too, love of country and the freedom to come here to church today.

This candle is a symbol of light; a symbol of God's love for all of us. He sent His Son to light our way. Christ said, "Follow me, I will be your guide."

Think of a great procession of people following Jesus as He holds a candle to light the way. Those who follow Him will not walk in darkness. They will not stumble or fall.

You only need to remember to "follow your leader."

"Christ says: "I am the light of the world" (John 8:12).

Sun, Moon and Stars

picture of a night sky
package of silver stars

Let us think today of some of the wonders of God's world. On the fourth day of creation, God made two large lights. He made the brighter light to rule the day. He made the smaller light to rule the night. He also made the stars.

The sun gives us warmth and light and makes the food and flowers and trees to grow.

Once a happy child said to her mother, "I feel like I have swallowed a whole bunch of sunshine." Did you ever feel like that? And did you want to share your happiness with someone else? The sun is a sign of God's love.

Do you think you could go out at night and look up at the moon and stars without thinking of God?

Once a mother was putting her child to bed. He looked out the window and said, "Mother, is the moon God's light?"

"Yes, dear."

"Doesn't God ever turn off His light and go to sleep?"

"No, God always stays awake to keep watch over us. He never sleeps."

The child snuggled deeper into the covers. "Then I need never be afraid while God keeps watch."

Another child asked his mother, "How much do you love me?"

"All the way to the stars and back," she told him.

You know how far it is to a star! That is how much God loves each of you.

The sun, moon, and stars are gifts of love from God to His children. Remember always to thank Him for His good gifts.

Would each of you like to put a star on this picture of the sky for someone you love very much?

"Praise him, sun and moon. Praise him, all you shining stars" (Psalm 148:3).

29

I Shall Not Fear

toy lion

Do you know what this is? It's a lion, yes. The lion is a fierce animal when it is hungry. It is called the king of beasts.

I am going to tell you today about a man who was a servant of God. The king had chosen this young man, Daniel, to be one of the princes in charge of his country. But some of the other princes were jealous of Daniel and planned to get rid of him.

They told the king what a great king he was. They said that he should sign a decree saying that if anyone asked anything of anyone but the king himself, they should be punished by being thrown into a den of lions. That ought to fix Daniel, they thought.

Those princes knew that Daniel asked God's help every day. So when the king had signed the decree, they spied on Daniel. When they found him at prayer, asking God to be his guide, they hurried back to the king.

They said to him, "You know what you said in the decree you signed. You can't go back on a decree, you know. This Daniel has asked something of someone besides yourself, so into the lions' den he must go."

The king was sorry for this because he liked young Daniel. But he couldn't go back on his decree, so into the lions' den Daniel went.

But that night the king couldn't eat or sleep. And the next morning he got up very early and went down to the lions' den.

Look at your watch and say, "But my time is running out. I must get on with the service. Ask your moms or dads what happened when the king went to the lions' den and cried out to Daniel. If they can't tell you the rest of the story, ask me another time. O.K.?"

> "I will not be afraid because you are with me" (Psalm 23:4).

What's in It?

can with label peeled off

What do I have here? A can. A can of what? What do you think is in it? How can you tell? Is there any way other than opening the can? No.

People are like this can in one way. You can't tell what is inside them by their clothes or how they look. A person may be dressed differently from you, have different hair or skin, or speak differently. But underneath, the person may be wondering how he can do something he very much wants to do, or how he can make someone like him. He may have dreams and problems and wishes, just like you, underneath a faded shirt.

I read recently about a country where people greet each other with signs. If you meet someone and he touches his lips as he passes, that means, "I will speak kindly of you." If he puts his hand over his heart, it means, "I wish you love and goodwill." But if he touches his own hand or your hand, it means, "I will do all I can to help you."

So the next time a new boy or girl comes to your school or neighborhood, don't judge him or her by how he or she looks or dresses. Like this can, you can't tell what is inside without getting to know him or her. You can't tell how nice a person is by just looking on the outside.

It's scary to go into a new school or neighborhood. Someday it may be your turn to move. Remember that, and be kind to new boys and girls.

"People look at the outside of a person, but the Lord looks at the heart" (1 Samuel 16:7).

31

Riddles

Bible
songbook

Good morning, boys and girls. Feel like guessing riddles this morning?

Well, then, why is a barefoot boy like an Eskimo? Give up? One wears no shoes and the other wears snowshoes.

How about this one? Why is a bad boy like a canoe? Both are paddled best from the rear.

How about, why is an anchor like a Christian? It holds fast in time of storm and trouble.

Let me tell you a story this morning about a boy named Isaac. His father had a large family to feed. They all had to pitch in and help. There was no time for playing.

Isaac liked to write poetry. So one day when his father found him writing poetry when he should have been working, he took a switch to him. As he was being punished, Isaac cried out in poetry, "Father, father, mercy take, And no more verses will I make."

But he did make more verses. God had a plan for Isaac's life. One Sunday morning, Isaac said to his father, "I think some of the hymns in our songbook are terrible."

His father replied sternly, "My son, if you would criticize, you must have something better to offer." And Isaac did just that. He wrote some hymns. And after three hundred years, we are still singing the songs that Isaac Watts wrote.

"Everything on earth, shout with joy to God!" (Psalm 66:1).

The Littlest Note

toy flute

I want to tell you a story this morning about a village where the people loved music.

It was such a happy little town that sometimes the birds flew in the open doors of houses to sing to the good housewives, who were too busy to be outside.

Once when the people had to choose between eating and music, they chose music. They sang as they walked along the roads. When they met a friend, they had to stop singing to say hello.

Well, one day word came that the great musician was coming to the village to play for the people on the organ of the church.

The people were excited. They sent for the organ tuner to come and check the organ because the littlest note had developed a bad squeak. *(Pipe the flute)* The organ man came. He played the big crashing notes first, then the wee little ones.

That evening the people all hurried to the church to hear the music. They all came early.

But something was wrong. The people who didn't know much about music, didn't know what it was. But others knew. The music was beautiful, but something was not quite right with it.

Of course, the great musician knew what it was. The organ man hadn't fixed the littlest note. He had taken the squeak out, but it didn't sing. It was only the littlest note, but it was important too. Without it the music was not complete.

When the great musician saw how disappointed the people were, he said he would come again and play for the people when the littlest note had been fixed. Then everyone went home happy. The littlest note would soon be fixed and the music made whole again.

It isn't size that makes things or people important. It's trying. Remember that, will you?

> "Sing a new song . . . " (Psalm 33:3).

The Rainbow

balloons
picture or sketch of the rainbow

What do we have in the bag this morning? *(Let some child take out the sketch)* What else is in the bag? Nothing? *(Let someone else look)*

Nothing else? Well, let me tell you something about the picture. Do you know what it is? Yes, a rainbow. Did you ever see one? Do you know what the rainbow means?

A rainbow is a promise. A promise of God's love and care for us. Always remember that when you see the rainbow in the sky.

Did you ever make a promise? Did you keep it? A promise that isn't kept isn't much good, is it?

God has made many promises to His children. Does he always keep His promises? Yes, always.

Once when the people of the world had forgotten God, He sent a great flood. You remember the story about the ark, don't you? How God told Noah to build it. How God had him take his sons and their wives and two of each kind of animal on the ark before the flood came.

Noah obeyed God and built the ark. Then the great flood came, but Noah and his sons and their wives and the animals were safe. And when it was over, God promised there would never be another flood to wipe out His people. Then He set His seal, the rainbow, in the sky to remind us of His promise.

(Give each child a balloon) These balloons are brightly colored like the rainbow. Take them home, and when you blow them up, let them remind you of the rainbow and God's love for each and every one of us.

"I am putting my rainbow in the clouds" (Genesis 9:13).

The Way

pair of children's shoes

It is getting near to the time of year when many of you will be needing new shoes for school. Does anyone have a new pair today? You do?

Do you know what kind of shoes Jesus wore? Sandles. At least during the hot time of year, He must have worn sandals as the people of His time did.

Some people called archaeologists dig in the earth to discover secrets of the time when Jesus lived. One time they dug up some little clay pots with a sort of spout on the front of them. But the strange thing about the pots was that they had curved bottoms so they wouldn't have set on a table.

What could they be? For a long time the archaeologists wondered. Then they discovered they were little lamps that were curved to fit the top of the foot. There were no flashlights in those days.

The roads were rough and stony. In the mountains there were only paths. And most people had to walk where they were going, if they didn't ride on donkeys. The paths were dangerous. There were places where it would be easy to fall.

So people made the little lamps of clay to fit over their feet. Then they filled them with oil and added little wicks. The lamps must have flickered as people walked, but they gave light to show the travelers the way.

We don't usually walk in such dangerous places at night anymore, but still we need to know the way we are going so we won't stumble and fall.

"Your word is like a lamp for my feet and a light for my way" (Psalm 119:105).

35

A Pattern

pattern
how-to book
Bible

(Show the pattern) Do you know what this is? A pattern, yes. Did you ever see your mother spread a pattern on material and cut something from it? The pattern showed her how to cut the cloth, didn't it? Did she ever make something for you? She used the pattern as a guide, didn't she?

(Show how-to book) Here we have a book that tells how to make *(kites, flowers of yarn, a birdhouse, etc.)*. Someone like this author, who knows how to do something, gives directions to those of us who need guidance.

Did you ever make something for your mother at school? Who showed you how? The teacher?

Who is the greatest of all teachers? Jesus!

He has given us directions on how to make our lives worthwhile. Can you tell me any directions He has given us, or patterns for us to live by?

Love God.

Love one another.

Be kind.

Obey your father and your mother.

Give thanks.

"If you do these things," Jesus said, "You will show that you love me."

God has given us a how-to book, the Bible. It's a book of directions on how He wants us to live. That is what we come to church to learn.

When you go home today, give your mom a big hug and tell her you love her. That will make your mom happy, you happy, and Jesus happy. Will you remember to do that?

"I will show you . . . " (1 Samuel 16:3).

He Loves Me

two daisies

Did you ever play the little game, he loves me, he loves me not, pulling a petal off a flower each time to see whether someone loves you or not? Of course, it's just a game.

You don't have to tear the petals off a flower to know that God loves you. He has told us over and over in His Book that He loves us and wants us to love Him.

And He doesn't love just some of us, or just some of the time, or when we are good. It makes Him sad when we are not good, but He loves us just the same. Each and every one of us.

Remember the time when many people were crowding around Jesus and His disciples said to the children, "You run along and play. Jesus is busy now."

But He wasn't too busy for them. He never is. He held up His hand and said, "Let the children come unto me. Don't send them away."

What a beautiful day it must have been. There were probably flowers growing all about and birds flying in the sky. How the children must have loved Jesus that day. It is one of the most beautiful stories in our Bible.

So let's take a flower and play a game today. As we pull the petals off this flower, say, "He loves you! He loves you! And you!"

Jesus loves the little children, and the ones not so little. He loves all the children of the world. He wants you to love Him, too.

"Let the little children come to me" (Luke 18:16).

Questions

jar of honey

I have a jar of honey in the bag today. Isn't it wonderful that suc
a small creature as a bee knows how to give us honey?

God's world is full of such wonders. Are there lots of question
you would like to ask sometimes?

One time a little boy named Randy had so many questions, h
couldn't get them all answered. Sometimes he felt he would po
like a balloon with all the unanswered questions in his mind.

"More questions, Randy," his mother would sometimes say. Sh
couldn't get her breath or find the time to answer them all.

Take the question about it raining on Saturday for instance. Hi
mother said that God had sent the rain because the ground wa
dry.

Randy wanted to ask why God had sent it on Saturday when h
wanted to ride his tricycle. Why couldn't God have sent it o
Friday? But his mother had answered the telephone, and Rand
had put that question away with all the others in his mind.

He wondered why God had made butterflies such beautiful co
ors when plain colored ones would have done as well? And ho
bees knew how to make honey from flowers?

And then one day at church school, Randy got the answers to
lot of his questions all at once. The words he learned didn't answe
all the questions he had stored up, but they helped him to answer
lot of them for himself.

The words Randy learned were, "For God so loved the world. .
He made seeds to grow because His children needed food. H
taught the bees to make honey from flowers because He so love
the world. He made it rain on Saturday because He knew that wa
the best day for the rain to fall. "For God so loved the world. . ."

"For God loved the world so much that he gave his only Son"
(John 3:16).

38

Answers

toy telephone

What is this? A telephone, yes. You can talk to people on it.

And did you ever think that God is as near as the telephone? He hears you when you pray.

Have you ever wanted something very much? Of course you have. Most everyone has. Did you ask your mother or dad for it? And did you get it? Do you always get what you ask for? Not always?

God tells us that He will always answer us when we pray. But He hasn't told us He will always give us what we ask for. Sometimes what we ask for is not best for us. He knows what is best. He always answers.

Let me tell you about a boy who wanted a horse. He thought he just had to have a horse for his birthday. So he told his father how much he wanted one. His father looked thoughtful and said, "We'll see."

As his birthday got nearer, the boy got more and more excited. He asked his father about the horse, and his father said, "I'm trying to think of the right answer for you."

On his birthday his father said, "Come and see what I have for you. The boy followed his father to the back porch. And there—no, there wasn't a horse on the porch. There was the liveliest, the cutest, the waggliest puppy the boy had ever hugged.

And his father said, "I know how much you wanted a horse, and I thought and thought about it. I think the puppy is the best for you. I didn't think you were big enough to take care of a horse.

The boy hugged the puppy and knew that his father had the right answer. That is the way it is with God too. He will always answer you when you pray. You may not get just what you ask for, but you will get what is best for you.

"I will answer them" (Psalm 91:15).

What Do I See?

hand mirror

Today we are going to play the looking-glass game. Look into this mirror and tell me what you see. Do you see a sad face? I should hope not. Do you see a happy, cheerful face? Do you see the face of a child who wants to be kind?

If you smile into the mirror, will the mirror smile back at you? Yes

God is a loving father. He wants His children to be happy. How do we know this? Well, the word happy appears in His Book around fifty times. And joy, another word for happiness, about a hundred and fifty times. And I don't know how many times the word blessed is used.

Children are happy people. You are God's helpers. You help to make the world happier. God wants you to be a friend and give joy to those about you. It has been shown over and over again that the way to be happy is to make someone else happy.

When you look in the mirror, you see someone who needs to love and be loved. Jesus has shown us how to be kind. He said we would be happy if we loved others too.

This week, I want you to play the looking-glass game. Smile at those you meet or play with or go to school with. See if your smile is not reflected or given back to you as though you were looking in a mirror.

Will you do that and let me know next Sunday how it worked? See you then. Keep smiling. God loves a smiler.

"Show us your kindness . . . " (Psalm 80:3).

Signs

various signs: Stop, Go,
Keep Off the Grass,
Beware the Dog

Can you tell me what this says? *(Hold up the Stop sign)* What might happen if you don't pay attention to it? It is put there for safety. Are children supposed to pay attention to it? Yes, they are! It's one of the first things you learn when you are big enough to go to school.

How about this one? *(Go)* It tells you when it's safe to go! And this one? *(Keep Off the Grass)* If you don't obey it, you may ruin someone's lawn or flowers that they spent a lot of time working on. You might even be charged a fine.

Now this one. *(Beware the Dog)* What does it say? And what might happen if you don't do as it says? You just might get bitten. That's right.

These are man-made signs for your safety and the protection of property. You saw signs on your way to church this morning. Stop signs. Street signs to help strangers find their way. And did you see a turn sign light blinking on the car ahead of you?

There are other kinds of signs, too. Did you see any signs of God's love for you on your way to church today? Trees. Flowers. Homes. A hospital. A church. A school. A field of corn. A rainbow. An apple orchard. Sunshine. Rain. All these and many more things are signs of God's love. See if you can discover others on your way home today.

"God also proved it by using wonders, great signs, and many kinds of miracles" (Hebrews 2:4).

41

Growing

measuring stick
cookies for only half of the class

Let's see, what do we have in the bag today? A measuring stick *(Or tape measure).*

Does your mother ever stand you against the wall and make a mark to show how much you have grown since the last time she measured you? Does she stand you with your back to your brother or sister or cousin to see who has grown most since last time? Does she ever say, "You're up to here on your daddy?" Does she say, "You're growing like a weed?"

Can you reach a drawer or shelf you weren't able to reach before? Yes, so you are growing in stature. *(That means tall)*

But there are ways to mark your growth other than how tall you are. Does your teacher send a card or record home to show how you are growing in wisdom and in your thinking processes?

There is still another measure to show how you are growing. That is in understanding and learning to live with others. In learning to share.

Do you get along with others better than you did when you were younger? Do you love others as Jesus has asked you to? That is surely a sign of growing. If your love doesn't keep up with your stature, you are going to be in trouble. It is sad to see someone growing taller, but not growing in loving kindness.

Let's see what else is in the bag this morning. Oh, cookies. But there are only enough for half of us. What shall we do? What do you suggest? Sharing? Very well, but will someone suggest how we can share our cookies?

"We love because God first loved us" (1 John 4:19).

Caring

pennies

I want to ask you a question this morning. How much are you worth? How much are you worth to your mother? If someone came along and offered her a million dollars for you, do you think she would take it? No, of course she wouldn't, because she loves you more than money.

How much are you worth to God? Even more than that. Because God loves you more than anyone can tell. Why else would He care for you as He does? Two of the Bible writers tell us that He sees and cares for even a tiny bird that falls. They add, "And you know that you are worth much more than the birds." He watches over you, and He knows your joys and sorrows, even when you forget Him.

Once when Jesus was talking about how much people are worth, He told them a beautiful story about a shepherd who had a hundred sheep and lost one of them. Did he say, "Oh, well, why bother about one sheep. I have ninety-nine others?"

Indeed, he didn't. He thought about that one little lamb out in the cold night, crying. And he went and searched until he found it. Then he wrapped it in his robe and brought it safely into the fold.

Then Jesus said, "God is like that shepherd. He loves each and every lamb of his flock. He is not willing that one of them should be lost. He loves us too much."

I would like to try a little experiment with you. I am going to give each of you _____ pennies. And I want to see if you can make someone happy sharing them.

O.K. Here are your pennies. Come and tell me next week how you shared them.

"We are his people, the sheep he tends" (Psalm 100:3).

Seeing

pair of sunglasses

Let's take a look at one another today. (*Put the glasses on*) You look different through these. But you aren't different, are you? (*Pass the glasses around*) Here, take a look for yourself.

These glasses make things look different, but they don't change things. There are some people who look at things "darkly" all of the time. They don't see the flowers because they are looking at the rain clouds. The rain clouds will make the flowers more beautiful, but those people don't think of that. They just think of the clouds. Do you know anyone like that?

It must make God feel pretty sad when He sees people unhappy even though He has given us so many lovely things to see.

It may be dark and gloomy and raining very hard, but an airplane pilot will tell you that you can go right up through a dark cloud and find the sun shining so brightly up there that it will make you blink.

There is another, easier way to make the sun shine on a dark day. That is by smiling. If you know someone who looks at the dark side of things, you can help to take his or her dark glasses off by smiling or doing some little act of kindness to remind that person of God's love in creating such a beautiful world.

Someone once wrote a story about a little girl who brought gladness to people by singing. People who wore dark glasses would hear her passing and feel glad because of her song.

"God's in His heaven,
All's right with the world."

The little girl's name was Pepita. You, too, can sing and make the world about you brighter. Try it this week and let me know next Sunday how it worked.

"Open my eyes to see the wonderful things in your teachings" (Psalm 119:18).

44

Thank You

envelopes with letters that
spell thank you

(Pass out the envelopes. Tell the children not to open them until they all have one. Then see who can put the scrambled letters into words first.)

Two of the most important words in our language are thank you. They are among the first words your mother taught you, aren't they? The person who doesn't learn to say thank you can never be very happy.

Thankful people are more loving people. They are kind. They want others to be happy.

Our Bible has a lot to say about giving thanks. Once when Jesus had made ten sick people well, one of them came back to thank Him. He said, "Where are the other nine?"

God is always helping, giving, loving, and doing things for people. How do you think He feels when they forget to say thank you? You would feel pretty sad, I think. You might even say, "Why bother with ungrateful people?" But God keeps on loving us.

Do you know of another way to say thank you to God? Think hard. Jesus said, "What you do for others you do for me."

When you do something kind for someone, it is a way of saying thank you to God. The psalmists of the Bible tell us over and over to say thank you to God for all His many benefits *(blessings)*.

When is the last time you thanked your mother for all the good things she does for you?

When is the last time you thanked God for the beautiful world He has given you?

Would you like to bow your head right now while we thank Him?

"Give thanks to the Lord" (Psalm 105:1).

Warm

pair of red mittens

Do you ever thank God for being warm? For clothing to keep ou the cold? Were you ever out in the wind and rain or snow and fe thankful when you got home again where it was warm?

Do you ever thank God for blankets? For furry places where ani mals can keep warm? For kittens and toast? For log fires tha crackle? For Moms and Dads and friends? For warm hearts an hugs?

Do you ever say thank you to God for spring and summer Winter can be fun, but wouldn't it be sad if spring and summe never came?

Flowers say thank you by blooming. Trees lift up their arms t the sun. Birds sing. Little creepy, crawly, hoppy things are thankf for holes in trees and in the warm ground. Bears are thankful fo warm caves.

Once when the collection plates were passed in church, a pair o red mittens was found in one of the plates. The minister held ther up and said, "These mittens have been found. Does anyone kno who they belong to?"

A little girl in the third row held up her hand. "I wanted to giv something too," she told the minister. "I had nothing else to give, s I gave my mittens. My grandmother made them for me, and the keep my hands so warm."

That is the kind of giving that makes God happy—giving from th heart.

Snuggle is a warm word. So is cozy. The Bible says, "Happy i the man who trusts in God." Happy is a warm word too.

Did you ever feel happy and warm because someone smiled you? You can make others happy by smiling. Try it this week.

"Thank him, and praise his name" (Psalm 100:4).

Christmas

Christmas candy

Good morning. I want to ask you a question today. Do you ever
ave dreams? Are they sometimes bad dreams?

I had a very bad dream the other night. I dreamed of a world
ithout Christmas.

Do you know how bad that would be? Can you think of some
ings we wouldn't have if there had been no Christmas night?

There would be no Christmas trees. No Christmas gifts. No
hristmas stockings to hang. No carols to sing. What else?

No baby Jesus. There would be no baby in Bethlehem. No shep-
erds or wise men coming to worship Him. No special Christmas
ar and no manger in a stable. Probably few people would ever
ink of love.

More than that, there would be no church or Sunday school.
hink what our towns and cities would be like without churches.

And there would be no schools. It was the church that started the
st schools in this country. They were started so that ministers
uld be trained to serve the churches. After that schools were
arted to teach boys and girls to read, so they could read the Bible.
ithout schools to train doctors, there would be no hospitals for the
ck.

I was glad when I awoke from such a terrible dream. And I'd like
s to sing a verse of "Away in a Manger" this morning. Let's be glad
r baby Jesus who came long ago and for the joy He brought. For
hristmas, the happiest time of the year.

"Give glory to God in heaven" (Luke 2:14).

Circles

pebbles

Can you tell me what this is? A stone, yes, a pebble.

Did you ever toss a pebble into a pool or a river and watch th circles spread out wider and wider until they reached the edge c the pool or the riverbank?

Well, the way we act is like that circle in the water. We say a kin word, or do something nice, and someone sees us and they want t do something nice, too. Or the kind word we say or what we d may reach out until it touches someone far, far away from where started.

We give money here in our church and it can reach out to hel feed a hungry child in Africa.

Once a poor little Chinese boy went singing down the stree every morning. A rich merchant heard him and asked his servar what the boy could be singing about. He was so thin and poor tha the merchant was sure he couldn't have enough rice to eat.

"I'm singing," the boy told the servant, "for those who do hav rice and for the day when maybe I will have rice too.

"What a foolish boy," said the merchant. But then one day th boy did not pass. And the merchant sent his servant to see wha had happened to the boy. He was at home, too weak from hunge to walk or to sing.

So the merchant said to his servant, "I miss the boy's singing See that he has rice enough to eat."

So the boy's song had reached out like a circle in a pond.

Jesus wants us to keep singing too. He wants us to reach ou that others in darkness may hear of Him. Send out the circle of you love. Drop your pebble in the troubled waters around you.

> "Send me your light and truth" (Psalm 43:3).